T0368366

Guided By Grace

Guided By Grace

Soul Winning & Miraculous Moments

Jack Giles

authorHOUSE®

AuthorHouse™
1663 Liberty Drive
Bloomington, IN 47403
www.authorhouse.com
Phone: 833-262-8899

Published by AuthorHouse 11/27/2024

ISBN: 979-8-8230-3840-9 (sc)
ISBN: 979-8-8230-3839-3 (e)

Print information available on the last page.

This book is printed on acid-free paper.

CONTENTS

PREFACE

THIS BOOK IS about true abundant life. A lifestyle that is full and complete can now be yours. The believer should ask for divine appointments every day. Someone once said, "Be bold and the mighty forces will come to your aid". This book is truly a miracle manual. As one obeys the Holy Spirit, miracles, signs, and wonders will become normal in your existence. Seize these stories and live with them. They will light a Holy fire in your soul, and you will never be the same.

INTRODUCTION

IN REVELATION 3:20, Jesus said, "Here I am! I stand at the door and knock. If anyone hears my voice and opens the door, I will come in and eat with that person, and they with me." The writer of this book heard the knock of Jesus and opened that door many years ago- Jesus came in and filled the empty place in my Pastor's heart.

Since that time, Pastor Jack Giles has dined with Jesus daily, feeding on the Word of God and listening to the whispers of the Savior.

Previously, Pastor Jack had been told that only parts of the Bible were true and some of the promises and miracles applied only to the early Christians, but then he read from Hebrews 13:8 – "Jesus Christ is the same yesterday and today and forever."

Yesterday, Jesus provided food for the hungry people, supplied money for the disciples to pay their taxes, delivered people from bondage, healed the sick, gave sight to the blind and restored hearing for the deaf. Jesus is the same today, and His miracles abound, as people trust the Savior and pray and believe.

This book reveals true miracle stories. The greatest miracle of all happens when you open the door and ask Jesus to come into your life. Today, in our troubled world, many people are lost and confused; they need to fill the empty place in their hearts with Jesus.

Today, you can even find Jesus at the local Walmart! This, because Pastor Jack is often there sharing the good news of the Savior. Read this book and learn how to share Jesus with others.

- Virgina Dawkins

MY METHOD IN SHARING CHRIST

THE HOLY SPIRIT, through the Apostle Paul says in II Corinthians 5.18-19 that all believers are given the ministry of reconciling others to God. In common language, God has planned for us all to be soul winners, are you one? How many soul winners do you know?

When we endeavor to be everything that God has purposed and planned for us, then we will exist with great satisfaction and joy. When we walk away from a person who has just prayed to receive Jesus Christ as Lord and Savior, your joy will be very great.

I want to walk you through how I share Christ with strangers. I do this in grocery stores, hospitals, hardware stores or whenever crowds gather. Everyone needs a plan as a method of operation. This works for me, you make the choice.

All strangers have potential. Some will die today or perhaps soon. There will be potential "Billy Grahams" or perhaps outlaws, all are important. All who are not saved are empty hearted and looking for something better.

Here is my plan! I look for individuals who are alone, male or female. My mode of operation is thusly, I smile and greet the prospect good morning how are you today? May I ask you a question? They always say yes! I would likely continue with a statement, I will most likely never see you again, are you a Christian? If they say yes, I encourage them with something positive. If they say no, I would continue with an observation. I would say to them, may I tell you something that I know about you? If they say yes, I then point to their heart and say this, it has been said that every person is born with a hole in their heart and the only thing that can fill that hole is Jesus Christ! I once was like that and know it to be true. Having that emptiness, I invited Jesus Christ to come into my heart and save me. This was the greatest decision I ever made in my life. Would you do this right now? I tell them how to pray and say almost everyone says yes. Then you lead them in a simple prayer inviting Jesus Christ to come into their heart as Savior. Almost every time I go into a big store, someone receives Jesus Christ. I leave with great joy. It has been said be bold and mighty forces will come to your aid.

Take a trip to Walmart today and the opportunity will be manifest. The last time that I visited a hospital to pray for a sick lady I said to a nurse, where is room 281? She pointed the way, "Oh by the way, are you a Christian?" I asked. She responded, "No Sir." Five minutes later, she prayed and received Jesus Christ! Opportunities are everywhere, Seize them!

Before my wife went to Heaven, she ordered groceries from Wal-Mart, and I would pick up those items at the side door. These groceries were always brought out by teenagers. When one chooses this method to get groceries the customer has the chance to encourage the youth in matters of spirituality and church attendance. Those witness efforts were always a joy because of the positive response that was evident. When one makes witnesses for Christ a priority everybody involved reaps significant blessings. The more that you do this your blessing becomes enlarged.

Let the reader understand my method in witnessing, after I talk to the person, I always gently instruct the individual in their prayer. Tell God that you know you were born with a hole in your heart and that you realized that Jesus is the only one who can fill that empty place. Ask Jesus to come into your heart and fill that emptiness with his presence. He will bring peace and power to the individual. This will be the best decision that they have ever made.

If the reader has never made this decision, now is the ideal time. Abundant life will be yours forever. A lot of empty hearted folks are waiting on you, in grocery stores, community events or other places. When folks gather you will be Gods answer for them. I guarantee, God wants to use you!

LADY SAVED OUTSIDE
REHABILITATION AREA IN HOSPITAL

I WAS WAITING TO enter this rehabilitation area of a local hospital where a lady about forty years of age was also waiting to enter this facility. I thought at first that she was an employee. I said excuse me Mam, may I ask you a question, sure she replied. Are you a Christian? No Sir, she responded, I shared with her how that I knew she had a big empty place in her heart! Yes sir I do, she responded. I shared with her that Jesus would fill that empty place forever if she would receive him. Yes sir I would like that, she said, and stood right there and invited Jesus Christ to be her Savior and Lord. Hallelujah!

SECURITY LADY GETS
SAVED IN WALMART

A COUPLE OF WEEKS ago I entered a Walmart store early on a Saturday morning. Just inside the store a lady security guard was eyeing all who entered the store. Good morning, Ma'am, I said to the eagle-eyed guard. How are you this morning? I'm fine, she replied. I say to her, may I ask you a question. Yes, was her reply. Are you a Christian? No, she stated. I pointed towards her heart and said, every person without Jesus has a hole in their heart. I once was like that! When I was seventeen years old someone told me that Jesus Christ could fill that empty place. I wanted that and asked Jesus Christ to save me. He filled my emptiness with his presence and peace. It was the best thing that ever happened to me. Immediately, she asked Jesus to save her. Amen!

SALES LADY GETS SAVED IN WALMART

I HAVE AN EXCELLENT 1997 Ford pickup truck. I learned about this vehicle from a young lady who used it to attend college. Well one night she hit a deer returning home from school. Across the front of the hood is a black strip called a bug shield. This item was ruined in the accident.

I went to Wal mart to purchase this important item. A young lady employee said that they carried this item, so I requested aid from the young employee. She declared that she would find this item for me. In the process, I asked her if she was a Christian. No sir was her answer. I shared with her how I was saved and how it wonderfully changed my life.

Would you like to have this happen to you? Yes, she replied. Right in the middle of that isle, she prayed to receive Jesus Christ.

WITNESS TO THAT MAN! I
HEARD THE HOLY SPIRIT SAY

DIVINE APPOINTMENTS ARE often strong and wonderful. I was headed into Rush Hospital when the Holy Spirit said to me, "Witness to that man sitting on the curb." It was sprinkling rain, and this man sat and said his addiction with was with cigarettes. May I sit and talk with you, I said to this stranger. Sure, said he, sit right here. After some small talk I said to this man, Sir are you a Christian? No sir was his reply. I pointed toward his heart and said every man has been born with a hole in his heart and the only thing that can fill that empty place is Jesus Christ. I know because I was like that, I was religious but empty inside because urged as a child to join the church.

When I was seventeen years old someone told me that Jesus could fill that empty place. I wanted that so I asked Jesus Christ to come into my heart and save me. He did, and it changed my life forever.

Sir, would you like to receive Jesus as your Savior, he said yes. He invited Jesus to come into his heart and save him. He looked into my eyes and said, "I have wanted to do that for a long time. Perhaps, someone today needs to pray for this also! You can pray for that right now and be saved!

CHURCH CUSTODIAN GETS SAVED

HERE RECENTLY A very young custodian came into my office with a vacuum cleaner as she tended to her daily tasks. I said, could we talk a moment? Sure, she replied. Are you a Christian, I asked her. I shared with her how Jesus saved me when I was seventeen years old. I relate that I attended church growing up and had been baptized much earlier, but no one had invited me to receive Jesus Christ into my heart. As an older teenager, I was encouraged to invite Jesus Christ into my heart, and I would be saved! I did and it changed me forever. Hallelujah!

A DIVINE APPOINTMENT
IN A PARKING GARAGE

EVERY MORNING, I ask God for divine appointments that day. I had just parked my truck on the third floor of Anderson Hospitals huge parking garage. There was not another vehicle within 80 feet of where I parked. Suddenly, a young man about eighteen years of age parked about 40 feet away. He got out of his vehicle and leaned against his truck and made a phone call. He then stayed there doing nothing.

I think to myself, this appears to be a divine appointment. I said, "hey, could we talk for a moment?" He walked over and I asked him, Sir are you a Christian? No, he replied. He then bowed his head and invited Jesus Christ to save him. Another divine appointment!

A SURGICAL MIRACLE

I RECENTLY HAD A skin cancer spot removed from my left cheek near my nose. The incision which was closed with stiches was almost three inches long. It looked absolutely horrible.

There were two miracles in this situation. First there was absolutely no pain after the stitches were pulled the gash together. The next incredible truth is that there is no scar on my cheek. No one would even realize there had been stitches in my face. Hallelujah!

A WONDERFUL MAGNIFICENT EXPERIENCE

YESTERDAY, I ENCOUNTERED the supernatural as few folks ever do. Every Saturday morning, I preach at a Christian rehabilitation facility called Righteous Oaks in Chunky Mississippi. I finished my sermon early because I wanted to get to a service at the Evangel Temple south of Meridian.

After leaving the facility I drove about a mile and suddenly I had a divine epiphany. My car and I were divinely transported within three miles of my destination.

In the Bible, in the book of Acts and chapter 8 verse 39 there is the story of a man named Philip who had an experience similar to mine. This man was normal physically and God transferred this person supernaturally. This incredible thing happened to me and my car yesterday as I headed to this church. How awesome is our God!

DIVINE APPOINTMENT IN A HOSPITAL

I WAS WONDERFULLY BLESSED in an elevator in Rush hospital in Meridian Mississippi several years ago. I said to the stranger "Excuse me sir, may I ask you a question?" "Absolutely," he responded.

I am a travelling salesman, he said to me. Then you have a lot of time to pray, was my response. Do you know what Luke says about prayer, I said to my new acquaintance. His response was please tell me about this scripture. In this scripture, Jesus talks about persistence in prayer, I shared with him.

We exchanged phone numbers and email addresses before he left. He texted me that night and said he helped someone that night in Tupelo Mississippi because of our conversation. I continued to encourage my new friend by sending texts in the following days.

The following Tuesday, I received an email from a member of my friend's Sunday school class telling me that the Sunday school class was blessed because of a meeting in the hospital.

I realized that my meetings with this brother was true divine appointment. This man is now a precious brother. Since that time, we have encouraged each other and shared several meals together.

I encourage each and every one to ask God for divine appointments every day!

CHRISTMAS TREE MIRACLE

M Y SON WAS reminded about a story long ago where they were protected by their Heavenly Father.

Christmas time has always been one of my most favorite times of the year. Growing up; Dad loaded us up early every December and we went Christmas tree hunting in the woods. Several gracious friends gave us permission to look for and cut down a Christmas tree on their property. The hunt was always so exciting. We always picked a beautifully shaped cedar tree. After Dad secured the tree in the house, we would decorate the tree with ornaments and lots of tinsel. One night after everyone had gone to bed; my brother Mark and I went and laid down under the edge of the tree. One of us had the bright idea to light candles under the tree. I remember thinking it was so cool! At some point we went to bed, leaving the candles burning. The next morning when my dad got up, he found where the candles had completely burned up under the tree without catching it on fire. This was truly a miracle! If you have ever seen a Christmas tree fire, you will never forget it. Apparently, God had plans for us, in these days we did not have smoke detectors. Thank you, Jesus, for your protection!

REPENTANCE IN A PARKING LOT

I NEEDED TO HAVE a couple of keys made on that afternoon. The nearest store to accomplish this necessity was on north hills street in Meridian Mississippi. I was getting my hair cut nearby anyways.

After accomplishing this necessity, I headed to my car. In the middle of the parking lot, I came face to face with a man about 35 years of age. "Can I ask you a question," He responded, "Yes sir." "Young man, are you a Christian," I asked, He said "Yes, but I am not the man I should be!" "Sir, if you will choose right now to become one, your entire life will be incredibly better." "You are right sir; I choose right now to live the life that God would have me to live."

A total stranger repented in the parking lot that day. Hallelujah!

EVIL SPRIT TRAVELS VIA PARCEL POST

M Y FRIEND JAMES received an unusual gift through the mail. His only brother was a couple of years older and had enlisted in a branch of the military. This branch or the service had sent the brother to an island in the South Pacific. The gift that James received was a mural about three feet wide and four feet long. The mural contained a picture of a Tiger and a big coconut.

This gift was hung up in the living room of his parents' home. About the time the gift was received, all sorts of accidents began to happen in the household. A neighbor's child was bouncing a ball in this room when it seemed to get out of control and knocked the mural off the wall and shattered the glass. The parents then took the object and put it in their barn.

Thereafter there was peace in their home, at some point, the mural was given to James who hangs it on his living room wall. All sorts of bad things begin to occur in their family. Upon a visit with his parents this strange happening was discussed with them. A family decision was made that the mural should be destroyed. Their decision was to burn the mural.

James laid the item on the ground in their yard and doused it with gasoline. When the item was completely ashes the visibility of the tiger was obvious. A feeling of unrest was in the air. James then took a stick and stirred the ashes and suddenly there was a release into the atmosphere.

There was now a sense of peace all around. The evil spirit had been vanquished!

JACK GILES

A FINANCIAL MIRACLE THAT WILL BLOW YOUR MIND

THERE ARE MANY promises in the Bible that are simply awesome. They are given to us by a precious Heavenly Father. Luke 1:37 is a prime example, For with God nothing shall be impossible. Another verse that is simply magnificent says that all things for which you pray and ask, believe that you have received them, and they shall be granted, in Mark 11:24.

My friend was an evangelist who preached literally all over the world. Their travels were widespread and expensive, so they faced an impossible financial future. What did they do; They prayed and their loving father made promises beyond their dreams.

They received an enormous gift from another country that was several hundred thousand dollars. There was simply no limit to where they could now minister. They personally shared this with me.

MY FIRST MIRACLE AS A PASTOR

I WAS PASTOR OF the Macedonia Baptist Church in Suqualena Mississippi when this occurred. The Pastor at the local methodist church was Everett Bonner; We were friends and often prayed together. He had a daughter who resided with her family in Mobile Alabama. This lady with her husband had come to visit the family when a crisis arose. The daughter had suddenly become very sick, and it was a holiday. The daughter said, Dad, call a church Elder and get prayers for me! We do not have one of those, said he, I will call my friend, Pastor Jack and ask him to come.

Having received this call, I went immediately to the methodist Pastors House. I poured out my heart for this lady and almost immediately vanquished every symptom of sickness in her body. My heart and that of my friends was greatly encouraged by what God had done. A new potential was released in my heart by this miracle. This was indeed a DIVINE APPOINTMENT!

SAVED FROM DEATH
AND HELL IN 1953

I WAS DRIVING MY brother's car and headed to the county fair near Philadelphia, MS. I was soon to be a Senior in my high school. My brother and two girls were occupants in the automobile. We lived in Daleville, MS near the edge of Kemper County. Somehow, I got elected to be the driver, but not familiar with the area, I got us lost. Realizing that I was on the wrong road, I made a U turn and almost got us all killed.

When I made the improper turn, I was unaware that a huge garbage truck was right behind me. To prevent hitting our car on the driver's side, the driver of the garbage truck swerved to the left and had to completely leave the road. Fortunately, he ran into fields and pastureland. No person or vehicle was damaged in the accident. The next February, I got radically saved in my Pastors car. Thank you, Jesus!

MY LITTLE SISTER
RECEIVES A WONDERFUL, MAGNIFICENT MIRACLE

WHEN MY YOUNGER sister was about six years old, she received from God a touch that can be described best only as a Divine Epiphany. My sister's name is Willie Mae. Suddenly, warts began to grow under her chin, all over her neck. My Mom took her to a well-known doctor for a consultation. His conclusion was not good. The only way to solve the problem was surgery, said he. The only drawback to this procedure was that scars would be evident permanently.

Our parents desperately searched for another plan of action. They were praying people, so pray they did. They were told that there was a black lady in Kemper County who was endowed with a gift of healing. She lived several miles southeast of the Oak Grove Community, they were told. On a Sunday evening, we all headed there seeking to find the answer to their prayer. Arriving at her home, we were told that she was at her church. We found the church and the Lady in question come to our car and talked with my parents. She did not have the gift of healing, which she graciously shared with my mom and Dad. It was noted that the Lady in question stared intensely at my sister's neck and was very compassionate, evidently a sweet, sweet spirit. About two days later, it was noted that her warts had disappeared! There was no residue on her gown or pillow. They had just disappeared and was an act of God! A miracle, plain and simple. Hallelujah!

CHURCH BIRTHED AFTER
DIVINE PROPHECY

A GROUP OF PEOPLE met together for the first time on Sunday morning June 29,1986. They had no name; they had just come to worship. They came again the next Sunday morning which was July 6,1986. They were meeting in Barbara Henson's nursery school, Kindergarten and Swim Gym.

A few weeks later this group chose to call themselves "The Church of the Way". The profoundly interesting thing is that Barbara Henson left a welcoming letter on the counter for this group on July 6, 1986. Mrs. Henson declared in this letter that God had let them know three months before that we would be coming. Barbara and Ralph Henson not only powerfully impacted this church but brought glory to God and the entire city by their lives. She knew God well enough to receive prophecy three months earlier.

This original letter is still in my possession, this letter was laminated for the sake of safety and to give glory to God. Hallelujah!

Copy of Letter:

July 6, 1986

Dear Brothers and Sisters in Christ,

You have been so gracious in thanking us for the use of the Gym that we feel we must share our hearts with you.

First; we want to thank you for assembling here for by doing so you are helping us to be obedient to our Lord Jesus. We consider that an extreme pleasure. How wonderful that the Great God who created the universe would choose to speak His will and allow us to share with you (a few hours each week) what belongs to Him in the first place. Ralph and I know as we look about this place, that what we see is not the work or efforts of mere mortals such as we, But all is His doing. Oh the Glory to hear His voice and to obey! Three months ago, He let us know that you would be meeting here, so we thank you for coming.

We do need your prayers, for we stand in awe of the task that He has set before us here. The care of and for the children. counseling with parents, and guidance of the 31 employees makes us a good candidate for your prayers.

We love you and count it gain that you are here.
In His Precious Love,

Ralph + Barbara

Ralph + Barbara

UNSAVED NURSE BECOMES
A CATALYST

A CATALYST IS AN agent of change! I was walking down a hall in rush hospital a few years ago when I had a divine epiphany that became a divine catalyst in my heart one night. I met a nurse coming my way that seemed in a hurry. I very politely asked her; Mam are you a Christian? She said no but I am in a hurry because of a doctor's order. I knew that I would never see her again. Suddenly, I realized that I needed a special treat or card to share with folks.

Two days later I designed a special card to share with folks in a similar needy situation. I have given away dozens now to folks in similar situations and even have shared with other churches who have started using them. God used an in a hurry individual an agent of positive change.

I probably may never see you again. Would you take a moment to read this?

It has been said that **EVERY** person is born with a hole in their heart. As a young man I was like that. My life was empty, meaningless and without purpose. Then, someone told me that Jesus Christ came to give me abundant life. **I ASKED** Him to come into my heart, and I was forever changed.

Behold, I stand at the door, and knock: if any man hear my voice, and open the door, I will come in to him, and will sup with him, and he with me.
REVELATION 3:20

YOU CAN DO THIS TOO. WILL YOU?
NOW? PLEASE!

Church of the Way   Pastor Jack Giles
601-604-3102

MIRACLES ON A MOUNTAIN

HIGH ON A mountain in southern New Mexico is a retreat center where people of all ages can have an experience with God. Quite some years ago my wife Joy and our boys were privileged to go there and be Gods catalyst for such an event.

The children were residents of south El Paso Texas. My sister was director of the south El Paso mission center. All the children were Mexican American citizens. There were around one hundred of these precious children and teenagers.

There were two worship and teaching sessions each day. Also, each day they had many fun games for everybody present. There were no invitations until the last worship service. At the end of the last time of worship, an invitation was given. During this time 49 youth and children received Jesus Christ as their personal Savior. Many tears and great joy were in all who were present. An overpowering of the Holy Spirit was experienced by all who were there! Hallelujah!

RHONDA BECOMES A CATALYST
FOR LIFE'S GREATEST MIRACLE

RHONDA HAS BEEN a friend for many, many years. When she was a small child, I had the privilege of praying for her when she was in danger of losing one of her arms. God saved her arm with a miracle.

A couple of years ago, Rhonda called me and requested I pray for a very aged acquaintance. The elderly lady was quite sick in a nursing home. It turns out that the precious sick lady tells me that she is not a Christian. We will have to call her more.

This dear lady was quite sick. As we talked, she admitted to me that she was not saved, but desired to go to heaven. She prayed to receive Jesus after I had prayed for her. This for me was a divine appointment. Rhonda in all was a divine catalyst in the situation.

AN AWESOME MAGNIFICENT
HEALING

CINDY IS A wonderful, faithful Christian lady. She is a retired schoolteacher, a profound help for hundreds or thousands of school children. She still helps many students who struggle in different programs to this day. A good mother and Grandmother is this lady.

Recently, she received a very, very great miracle. Cindy had begun to have internal stomach pains. Cindy gave in and went to the Doctor and had test ran. The medical report showed that Cindy had eleven ulcers in her stomach; the report further showed that also there were two black spots in the mix. Her son Todd called me and requested prayer for his precious Mom and shared her phone number with me.

I called and prayed for this very concerned lady of God. Soon after this prayer, Cindy went back and was re-checked by the same Doctor. The report showed all 12 ulcers and dark spots had all vanished. The doctor said he had never seen a miracle like this before.

TESTIMONY OF CURTIS

WHEN I WAS growing up, I was told, "You is sorry and no good. You ain't never gonna mount to nothin!" Those words stayed with me, and I started getting into trouble at an early age. After I swore never to go to jail Satan attacked my mind trying to get me to take my own life, but God would not let that happen.

The Lord brought me out when I couldn't see my way out. Once I came out of darkness into light, I prayed never to go back; I sat in church and prayed. I was so tired of living like that, but once more I got off track. My family and everyone I loved turned against me.

I came to Meridian and lived in a homeless shelter. It was there where I overheard a gray-haired minister counseling a tenant who was suicidal. I will never forget the words of the minister who spoke to them. Pastor Jack Giles was speaking of God's hope for me!

Pastor Giles invited me to his church, and I began attending services there. One day in that church, I heard a sermon on the importance of forgiveness, and I realized that even though I had received Jesus's forgiveness for my sins, I had not forgiven the people who had hurt me. I walked down the aisle for prayer, and I prayed to forgive my enemies.

Because Christ is my Savior, I am no longer alone nor homeless. Today I have much hope. I know that nothing or nobody can separate me from the love of God.

- Curtis

DEMON HIDES IN A CONSPICUOUS PLACE IN A HOME

FOR MANY YEARS I was involved actively in a ministry of exorcising evil spirits. I did this probably hundreds of times in lives or homes. This was a highly successful ministry. My wife and I became acquainted with a lady who believed that her apartment was inhabited by an evil spirit. Objects would be moved around at night when she would be sleeping.

The picture frame involved was 23x36 inches and very expensive. My wife Joy and I came to believe that the picture itself was inhabited by a dark spirit. Our conclusion was that the frame could be saved while the picture itself was destroyed. We went to the lady's home and took the frame from the picture. The picture itself was burned after separating the two.

After this transpired there was peace in the apartment, no objects moved again in this home. There was absolute peace thereafter. We were in their lives to bring peace, and it was permanent.

A LOCAL DOCTOR GETS
WONDERFULLY SAVED

SOME OF MY readers will be amazed and surprised at the tale of this story. At least 40 years ago this gentleman's wife called at six thirty in the morning. She said my husband just came from the hospital and said he is never going back.

He is now in heaven, but then he was a beloved Deacon and Sunday school teacher. I said to his wife, put the coffee pot on, we are going to need it, you are in a spiritual battle. You are an excellent Sunday school teacher and your husband who is a greatly respected leader in your church, an act of your will, you need to forgive the person who greatly offended you.

My friend talked and prayed about what had transpired that morning. We remained friends and he finally returned that same morning to the hospital. Later he went to heaven while still a respected Deacon in the church. The unfortunate news was never mentioned again. I had numerous visits with him and his wife in the ensuing years.

This local Doctor was wonderfully saved on that unfortunate day. All of us experienced the manifest presence during those challenging hours.

THE ROLEX WATCH

ANOTHER UNUSUAL MIRACLE involved a genuine Rolex watch from a man. This individual was a precious man of God. He came to me and said, I have a Rolex watch that I want to give to you; You can keep it or sell it, whichever you choose will be fine with me.

At that time our school, Kings Academy, needed money, so I chose to sell the watch and bless the school with the proceeds. The Rolex watch brought in eighteen thousand dollars to help our school. Praise God!

FINANCIAL MIRACLES

THERE IS ABSOLUTELY no limit to the way God brings miracles to his needy children. A central issue in the lives of all believers is money. This is true individually and corporately.

Our church once had a thoroughly successful school called Kings Academy. It was both an elementary and high school. Our church had a wonderful lady member who had a business in our town. In the center of this business, she had a table surrounded by tons of chairs. On the table was a coffee pot that was constantly brewing. Good coffee and uplifting conversations were always present.

On this occasion, the lady in question opened a box containing a beautiful diamond ring. This she said, I am giving to our school to help with a pressing financial need. At that time there was a lady in town that owned twelve businesses in Mississippi. Someone kept on pressing that I go by her business and show her the ring.

I went by her business office and introduced myself and gave my reason for being there and was received by the Christian lady. She immediately looked at the ring through a jeweler's eye. She immediately said, "I will give you nine thousand dollars now for this ring!" I graciously refused and asked her to reconsider. "Get your best offer and come back," she said to me.

A few weeks later, I went back to her office and said, "I need to sell this ring today". The jeweler replied, "Okay, I will give you eleven thousand dollars". I said "No"! Her husband spoke up and said, "Give this man eleven thousand five hundred dollars". Immediately she gets her check book and writes a check for twelve thousand five hundred dollars to Kings Academy. I said thank you Mam and thank you Jesus! This was a divine appointment.

NAN'S MIRACLE

A LONG TIME AGO when I was young and foolish I tried smoking. I loved it, when I was in college it was not uncool for girls to smoke; most of my friends smoked also. I started dating my husband when I was a sophomore in college, and he was a senior in med school. We had grown up on the same block and he had taught me how to ride a bike when I was five and he was ten. He hated smoking. I am very ashamed of this, but I continued smoking for years but never around him.

I prayed and prayed for years that God would help me quit, but it seemed to me to be no avail. Finally, I went to a spirit filled conference in North Carolina led by Judith and Francis McNutt. On the third night there was a healing service; I was sitting in the front row. Francis told us that when they went to primitive countries where the people had much less sophisticated belief systems that the all-powerful Holy Spirit would be so strong in the meeting that the unholy spirits or demons would manifest and leave. The people would clap and praise God.

Francis don't tell us what you need, Judith and I will pray in the Spirit and God will show us what to pray for. As they prayed, most everyone they prayed for fell to the floor. Soon some who were on the floor began manifesting. I had never seen this before and to me it was really scary and grotesque. I was very upset. I was told that most of those who were delivered of evil spirits had in some way been involved in the occult.

I had heard that Jack Giles in Meridian had a deliverance ministry. When I got back home, I called and made an appointment to get him to pray for me. If there was anything like that in me, I wanted it out!

Pastor Jack interviewed me, asking me questions about myself and I told him about my smoking problem. He and his wife, Mrs. Joy, prayed for me for a while, then I left. I still wanted to smoke so I did. Three days later my husband and I were in the den- I think we were both reading. All of a sudden, I felt this heat go through my body from my head to my toes. I knew it was the Holy Spirit at work in me. About that time, my husband got a beep and had to go the hospital. The thought went through my mind that I could go out on the porch and smoke. Immediately I realized that I didn't want to smoke, and I haven't had or wanted a cigarette for years and years.

Jesus said he came to set the captives free. Indeed, he set me free from that sin that is so repulsive to me now. I am so, so thankful!

AN UNUSUAL MIRACLE PROMPTED
BY THE HOLY SPIRIT

I WAS IN MY office at church one day when an outstanding local Pastor came by for a visit. We prayed together about the mutual concerns of both churches. The man was one of my best friends.

As I was getting ready to leave, my friend declared, "as I was driving by, the Holy Spirit said, stop and let Pastor Jack take authority over this issue in your life, So, I am here to obey God." In the bible's book of Matthew chapter ten and verse one, Jesus gave his disciples authority over unclean spirits, to cast them out! I proceeded to command the spirit troubling my friend to leave! It had no choice but to leave and depart it did, immediately!

ADDITIONAL BOOKS BY THIS AUTHOR

FASCINATING MIRACLES IN the Life of a Country Preacher – A Faith Inspiring Chronicle Incredible Treasures Awaiting Discovery – This book is a compilation of carefully researched stories about buried or hidden treasure. Twenty-one accounts of monetary treasure and two narratives of spiritual wealth are chronicled in this writing. The reader will be intrigued by the possibility of personally finding treasure. It is entirely possible that all who follow the directions in this manual will become incredibly wealthy. Paul Ott Carruth calls this book a treasure map and Rev. Mike Boles declares it to be a "masterpiece."

Unmasking Guerrilla Warfare in the Church - This book considers the seriousness of intolerance, bigotry, prejudice, and racism in the church of Jesus Christ. The beauty of the book is that an effective, workable solution is offered for the problems. Dr. Fred Wolfe calls this a powerful book, full of truth that must be heeded and obeyed. Jack Taylor, a noted evangelical, believes this book will be important to the twenty-first century.

Jesus Christ Still Heals – A book that shares the miracles and testimonies that would inspire anyone.

ACKNOWLEDGMENTS

I CONSIDER THIS TO be the most important book that God has given to me! The reason is that I am encouraging folks to share Christ as a routine matter.

Church of the Way – The entire Church family has encouraged and prayed for me. Thank you to each and every one of you.

Todd & Dee Dee McCormick – Thank you to Dee Dee who did all the typing for manuscript and Todd for running errands for this project.

Tony Boutwell – Thank you to Tony for designing the front cover.

Joe and Cindy Giles – Thank you to both for being a great help with this project.

Michael and Kathy Giles - Thank you to both who have also been an encouragement.

Virginia Dawkins has also greatly encouraged me.

Thank you to Jesus for putting this project in my heart.

Printed in the United States
by Baker & Taylor Publisher Services